Ethereal Tales

Brenda da Silva

BookLeaf Publishing

Presentation by *BookLeaf Publishing*

Web: www.bookleafpub.com

E-mail: info@bookleafpub.com

ISBN: 9789357697101

First edition 2023

DEDICATION

To all of those that can't help but daydream
about love

ACKNOWLEDGEMENT

I would like to thank those that read my poems when they were just a mix of words without meaning and no rhyme scheme. You are the reason why I dared to publish this collection. I want to thank one in particular for being the main reason why many of my poems exist. You know who you are. I love you.

Silver and gold

He was a breeze of a chilly morning air
So comfortable in being cold
She was too much of summer even to care
Everything she touched turned into gold
She believed his ice heart, with her heat, would melt
Craving the winter, even with the morning darkness to dwelt
Guardian of a secret in her lips color red
Fighting for him, not worried if she would end up dead
Stuck in a world of unfolded truths and dark lies
He was the only one that could see past her eyes
Even if he was too far away in a world where the sky was too high to touch
And wanting was not enough
In need of each other but too afraid to dare admit
She just needed him to commit
To accept her love and her hands to hold
She was willing to welcome the cold
Wondering if he could handle the heat
Pondering if he would leave after he saw her reality
Schemes and frauds were normal to her
Dirty money covered in fur
She always knew she was different than the most

But was she just a ghost?
Immune to the bad reputation
Could she even be sorry for her situation?
Was she being selfish by dragging him into such
a complication
Or was she just a lover outside the devastation
He took her out of her misery
Together they decided they could indeed change
history
Allowed her warm hands to hold the cold
Silver and gold
Both broken for years
With eyes full of tears
Both were put together in months
They could be seen as drunks
From love too great to be untold
So this is how their story unfolds

Epiphany

Seemingly, it was love at first sight
Waiting for you to be my long-lost knight
Entirely lost in our conversations that last
through the night
Indeed, I can say I believe I was right
You gave me a story that inspired me to write
Even when the probabilities were not on our side
And I beg the moon and the stars to shine
And for you to never leave me when the clock
hits midnight
Be with me now
And forever, I will allow
To our love bow
Let me get lost in my thoughts
Turn every corner of my mind
For your eyes to find
Let me scream your name
To you, deeply surrender my soul
As I know, your arms as the only place I feel
whole
Let me chase my dreams
With your heart as the only thing I hold
Enchanted by the love that felt like gold
Let me close my eyes and sleep
Only to haunt you in my peace

Waiting for the fire to cease
Let me love you more than I do write
Words on a paper aren't deep
But those tattooed on your lips
Let me be yours and no one else's
Seal the deal
Feel the feel
My love, everything is real

Written in the stars

I sometimes believe the universe sends us gifts
Once with eighty-eight constellations
Millions of stars that, together, create a
connection
Millions of stories point to a direction
One of them I took as my own gift
So its name was mine to give
I decided it was easy to nickname it ours
And waited for it to unfold my desires
To tell the story of you and I
And how we met when I couldn't deny
The help only you could provide
Such a strong connection
I simply could not ignore
How it felt like our story was written for us
Something that only destiny herself could
articulate
How it all started with an empty conversation
When I didn't even allow my imagination
To believe such heat resulted from twin flames
Shining like our star
Revealing who we are
Together with fingers intertwined
We admire the shimmering future ahead of us
Written in the starry sky

Lighting up the pitch
Together we are art
Together we are myths
Together we are legends
Together we get scared by the infinite
possibilities of the future
Afraid they will push us away
Our story belongs to fate
But it is ours to live
Whispering prayers to the stars
And getting back sighs of comfort
Our story is written in the sky
Just look, live and wish
The universe will answer us
And if needed, more constellations will create
Because it's you and me
And that nothing can change

Words I long to write

You became the poem stuck in my throat
So deep in my thoughts
Making me unable to translate it into words on a
paper
I share this secret alone
I carved it in my soul
Your silence becomes familiar
Your answer is the words that I am most scared
to read
In my head, I fantasized
So from the anxiety, I can hide
Fantasies of the warmth of your hugs
Creating a scenery where I want to live in
Whenever I dare to ask you
Would you please consider me?
I fear I will never find such courage
It is safer to hide my feelings
Until suffocating, they become
I would never dare to ask you to love me
But I beg you to look at the stars
And wonder why I'm not in your arms
And maybe you are unaware that on the other
side
In the solitude of my mind
With pen and paper in hand

With words finally filling the void
I look at the stars and wish
I humiliate myself before them
Begging for you

Rebel

I have a confession
I am passionate about the idea of love
A feeling that is known for its devastating
character
The only one capable of changing all my beliefs
No planning, right time, or the exact moment
Ideas of the future, once uncertain,
Shape themselves in genuine certainty
Confessions were written in the secret of paper
and pen
So loud, but only two people can hear it
So visible, but only two people can see it
So consuming, but only two people are
completely consumed
Secret promises that come true
Midnight conversations that inspire
Symphonies that reflect the feelings
The rebellion of someone who always followed
the rules
The madness of someone who always sought the
solitude
The anguish of someone who always chose
safety
The passion stemming from the idea of your
love

Just yours
My first, only, and last act of rebellion

Addicted to you

Freshly ground beans
A cup of hot coffee offered to me
Warm on the hands
Tender to the heart
Intensively bitter
Intoxicating scent
Absorbed by my soul
Memorized by my mind
Like a splash of milk
I sought to soften your intense essence
Life, with all its bitterness
Like small cubes of sugar
I thought about the sweetness of your existence
Like delicate vanilla
I ought to change the taste of your sadness
But the unmistakable intensity
The strongest of the scents
Permanent in my life
Still present, following my imagination
The bitterness that I can still taste
Believe me, I'm addicted
To your taste
To your scent
To you

The muse and the artist

On the shelf of my heart
All the books became about you
The ink that runs through my veins
Restrained just for our story to write
With my mind full of the most beautiful words
I give my hands the function of transforming
them into poems
Even with the immense amount of pages torn
out
And other artists are trying to smear our
scriptures
To defame the one who awakens pure art in me
I still wanted it in my literature
Nothing ever stopped the rising inspiration
My writing added you to my life's story
Knowing that some people are just phrases
Other commas and periods
But you are much more than a chapter
The lines written about you multiplied
Impossible to ignore the book that became yours
My words that suddenly could only be called
your own
There were old books that I forced myself to
close
And people that I forced myself to forget

And then I found you
And I came across the inevitable
Knowing that even with the old stories
You would become the only one
Who I would want to write my story with

I will see you in my dreams, darling

Like a dagger stuck in my chest
Distance and uncertainty pierce beyond my flesh
Longing and desire reach my soul
For our love, there would be no Capulets or
Montagues
From the family that might try to keep you apart
I would defend you with all my heart
From your lips, I would drink the poison
So that I could touch them
For you, I would learn the language of sonnets
And in our secret encounters, I would hold them
as promises
Hoping the starlight is not the only one kissing
my skin
You need no invite for me to let you in
On my balcony at midnight light
Your face lights up the dark
My gaze seeking the peace in your brown eyes
Forgetting about the hate and the fear
In secret, love reappears
I try to remind myself of the challenges I will
face
But looking at you, I can just know I would
follow you to any place

For your arms to become my home
No amount of barriers would hold me away
You are the only one I will ever chase
Knowing that in this life, I love you deeply
And in death, I will find him dreaming eternally

Broken a thousand times

Resting in your hands
My book of pain
Read to you every page
Lost in the words
Where I confess my fears
The key to my most valuable belonging
Tattooed in your fingertip
You open my heart
Turn over my feelings
Destroyed my barriers
Made promises with no intention to keep
Showed me your body heat
Wrapped me until your arms felt like home
You loved me like a coward
Leaving me alone and deceived
You gave me a fairytale with no happy ending
But in the hands of a dreamer
It felt like a tale as old as time
A girl that never expected you to leave
With the lips that you kiss with the sweetest
venom
Leaving only the pain of the absence
Broke the fragile heart
Shatter it into pieces

A hopeful heart, even after years of inflicted
pain
Your love now has a sour taste
Your departure served as an answer
To the silent question tattooed on my lips
If not you, who is going to stay?

Dreamcatcher

I dream of kissing the sky
But will I ever be able to fly so high?
If I ever dare, I hope your eyes find
And in the softness of your lips, hide
Willing to confront the desires only you can
satisfy
Let me at least try
Try to forget you were ever on my mind
Try to erase the pain that made me blind
But without you, I leave my heart behind

I still dream of kissing your scars
Realizing that I wish for you upon the stars
My love, I can no longer deny
It is painful trying to put my feelings aside
When my heart to yours is tied
Let me at least love you right
Love your beautiful thorns
Love you through the storms
Love you in all forms

I dream of kissing the sky with you
I dream of kissing the marks that made you blue
Would you hold my hand and fly somewhere
only we know?

Would you allow my hands to touch the snow?
I promise I can handle the cold
I promise I will be by your side when we turn
old
I will tell you stories that have never been told
I will turn the damages into pure gold
My love, I am here, and I am genuinely yours to
hold

Frame

With him as a witness
Of the most terrible of my crimes
I face the pressure of all the accusations
If meeting him in eternity was the only
consequence
I would face the tribulations
And the sleepless nights
The days of endless tales
Moments that are now part of my history
No accusation will ever make me reconsider
The crime I most wanted to confess
The secret that became the hardest to keep
Not noticing little by little his heart I was
stealing
Different from before, becoming the only
outcome
I became forever marked by his promises
Chained to all the unforgettable sonnets
Unable to escape your sweet rhymes
The Prison of eternal love
The verdict that waits for me
Maybe it's not so terrible after all
If the crime that condemns me is to love him
until the very last call

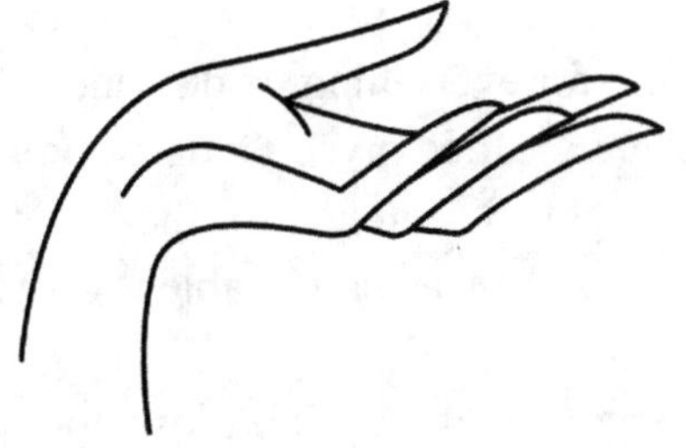

Broken bottle of pills

The label on the bottle promised me solace
And I had no idea what that would cost me
It solved all my problems, don't you see?
I am being careful, I promise
Except it feels like dancing with evil
Expecting to leave hell but still holding his
hands
And falling for everything he demands
And I proudly called myself a daredevil
So many nights, I searched for the sweet taste
I never realized I was barely able to survive
without it
I told everyone they shouldn't lose control, what
a hypocrite
Telling me to stop was a time waste
Addicted to the substance
It gave me peace when there was trouble
It made me so comfortable in a bubble
The side effects had no importance
I had to be free from the sweet
I knew in the end, one of us would win
And I found the strength not to give in
But my heart ached at every beat
A constant fight
The temptation of opening the bottle

Believing it will get easier little by little
Questioning if I will be able to sleep at night
And every night, I do
Waking up the next day
And dealing with what my anxiety has to say
The pain needs to be felt. You believe in that,
don't you?

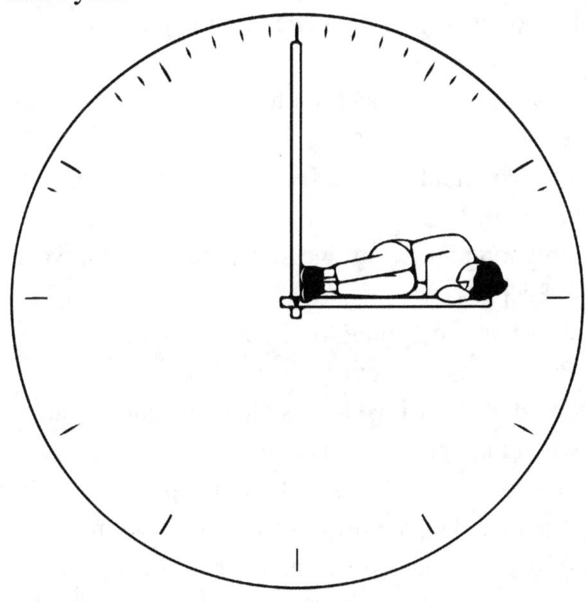

Nemesis

My mind is my worst enemy
The reflection in the mirror is my biggest
nemesis
I sabotage myself by believing the tales of my
legacy
Always a naive girl running away from her soon
reality
Will you hold my hand to drop it close to the
precipice?
How long until you find someone new you want
to keep?
When are you going to discover that my
company is not your favorite?
I read all your love letters trying to find a clue of
when I am going to savor it
I can't find words that cut that deep
Where is the pain they always promised me?
Why does your love taste like honey?
Am I finally breaking the curse led by money?
I pray you are the one to see me for me
To save me when the war finally erupts
Running away with me from the reality of
corrupt
But my mind is still my worst enemy
Making me wait for the time you decide to leave

My forever

Forever, for me, always sounded like impossible
A trail of failed marriages I followed
Love with the taste of failure, I swallowed
Always believing my love was doomed to be
invisible
Or discarded at the first sign of pain
Constantly questioning if I was ever capable of
rain
When the desert on my chest made me miserable
Would you take away the bad memories
And replace them with beautiful stories
Show me your love for me can be unconditional
I'll promise my love for you will not be
measured
Even when not a single star in the sky shines, we
stay together
Even when not a single soul wanders the land,
my love will be reciprocal
Even when not a single drop of water fills the
oceans, by your side, I will remain
Even when not a single planet survives, my love
won't be in vain
Even when not a single word comes out of my
lips to declare what my heart will forever hold

I will repeat a thousand times for now until we
turn old
Even when not a single beat of my heart can be
heard
Know that in another realm of reality, you don't
have to say a word
Forever, for me, always sounded like impossible
Until you came into my life, simply unstoppable
Forever by your side sounds right
And my love for you will go beyond this life

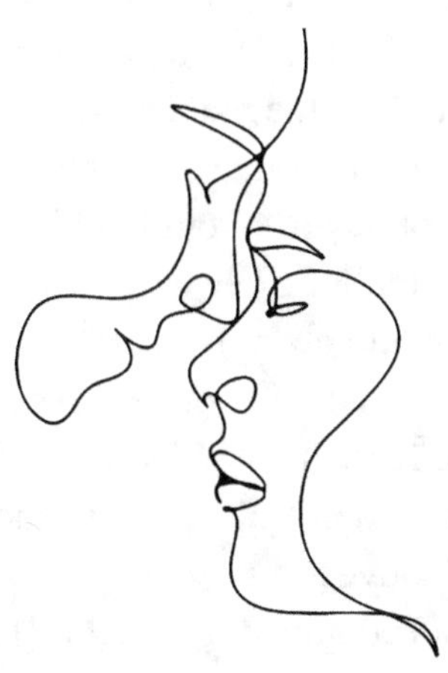

Sweet

Love tasted bittersweet
Nothing that would make her heart skip a beat
They looked at the gold
And forgot about her soul
Tried to win her heart
By tearing her apart
Their eyes could only focus on the green
Ignoring the desires of the queen
She did not fall for the princes
Or the warriors with imperious glances
She did not fall for the magicians
Or the curse breakers that feared her conditions
She did fall for anyone from her kingdom
They started doubting her wisdom
A dreamer should never be a queen
But her true wish could not be foreseen
A cursed life for someone that longs for love
The doubt that she would find the one to look
for the stars above
Was there indeed hope for someone like her?
Was there anything they could do to deter?
She was utterly delusional about the idea of an
ardent love
She was entirely dreaming about the idea of an
innocent love

Until he showed up
He filled with passion her empty cup
Looking at the queen, he saw the girl underneath
Realized how difficult it was for her breath
So he gave her air
Looking at the queen, he saw what no one else could see
A girl that just wanted to be free
So he took away the heaviness of the crown
Looking at the queen, he saw beneath the curse
The magic was undone, and he could see her worse
So he stayed by her side
And promised never to leave her life
He stole the keys to her heart
And suddenly, love tasted just sweet

Nice meeting you

It was always easy for me to picture my future
I could just close my eyes and see 10 years from
now
I would have the job I always wanted
The purses I always desired
The body I starved to have
The kids I never believed I could actually take
care
The husband that would use me from time to
time
The car I would drive to therapy
The perfect family through the lens of a camera
The meals at the table drowning in silence
The holidays I would pretend to like
The family gatherings which not attending was a
crime
The friends that were just as fake as my reality
A life I was miserable but destined to have
It was easy because it was my only option
Misery was my destiny
It was my future
It was my reality
But then suddenly everything changed
Picturing 10 years from now became so hard

Accepting a life that I had not signed up to have
was a burden
I could have different dreams
And be motivated by different goals
Use my voice that had never been heard
Follow my wishes that had always been ignored
I saw my future through different lenses
And it all became so hard
I had to change
I had to move
I had to hide
And I had to fight
So I did
When I found you

– my new self

Eternally

You learned how to hide your scars
Like kids your age were taught to shoot for the
stars
You discovered the best places to hide
While kids were outside exploring during a bike
ride
You realized that the world was evil
Forgetting that a kid like you should have no
idea about the true devil
You were raised to believe you were not meant
for love
And you could never touch anything from the
above
That little kid that went through so much
Grew up not wanting anybody's touch
He distances himself from everyone
So far away but still shined like the moon and
the sun
I was mesmerized by the glow
Something in you whispered and convinced me
to go
Go towards you
And with my bare hands, touch through
The glass that would cut anyone's hands
But hold mine like we were long-time friends

I saw your scars
And connected each one of them like they were
my constellation of stars
You took me to the places you used to hide
And I started seeing the world through your eyes
You confessed the evils that haunted you
through the years
And I promised you I wouldn't leave even if
there were tears
I never taught you how to love
You learned by yourself
And told me that I came to your life like a dove
And there was no way you could love anybody
else
I whisper promises I will do everything to keep
And you memorize my words until you fall
asleep
As my hands brush through your hair
I know I am no longer scared
I will love you even after death
I will care for you until my very last breath
Be by my side until I am gone
And I will love you like the moon loves the sun

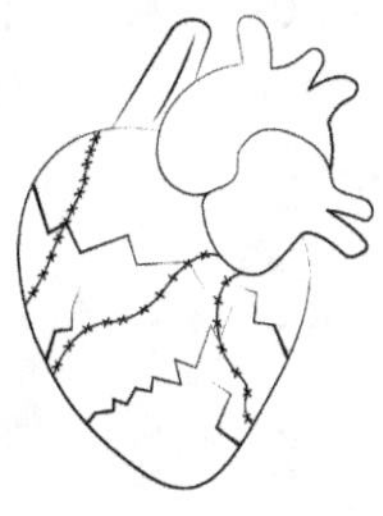

Changes

I never really understood watching three movies
in a row
Until I meet you and would watch a thousand if
you ask
I was always scared that nobody would stay to
watch my garden grow
But you promised not to leave even the trees
have no leafs

I never wanted to leave my comfort zone
Until you asked me to eat sushi as your birthday
gift
It terrified me that nobody wanted to hear a
word of my own
But you memorized every detail about me while
listening to Taylor Swift

I hated the feeling of ups and downs of life
Until you felt like home when times get hard
I believed love would feel like I got stabbed by a
knife
But you stole my heart during the second I let
down my guard

The reflection of my insecurities dominated my
reality
Until you appeared and changed the course of
my fantasy

Awake

When two broken souls meet
It feels like the galaxy explodes
Like the sun and the stars collide
Forming a bond that no one can divide
Getting addicted to the taste sweet
Forgetting about the world and its cruelty
Both playing a dangerous game
But for that love no one was to blame
They felt like kids fascinated with beauty
Attempting to run away from their demons
And wishing upon the stars
For their fairytale to start
Afraid that this whole they were just dreaming

I will always choose you

I won't always be the easiest choice
And my name definitely wasn't the first whisper
in your voice
I have my share of flaws and mistakes
That I tried so hard to hide for your sake
Miles away and oceans apart
How can I still be the one holding your precious
heart
Please don't leave when the sun doesn't shine
When all the concealed darkness crosses the line
I won't always be the easiest choice
But I promise you I will always be there as an
option
I will be there when you are scared
                    when the war is declared
                    when there is peace for us
                    when we are nothing but
dust
I will hold your hand for every second of bright
daylight
But I will have you even closer in my arms for
the cold nights
I won't always be the easiest choice
But I am willing to keep choosing you

Hoping that it will be easy for you to choose me too

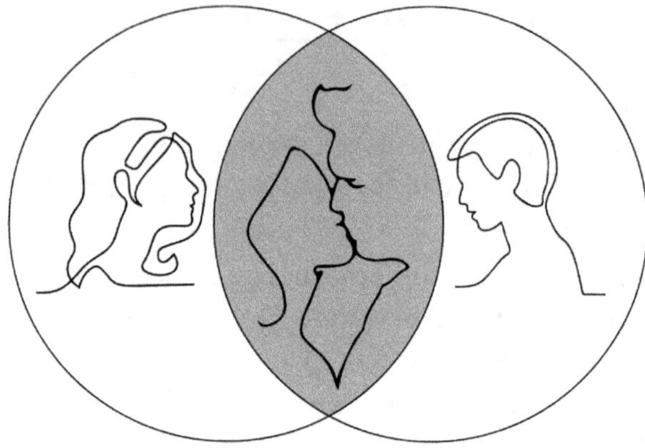

You

You are the songs that you listen to when
nobody is near
The thoughts that you speak loud and clear
And the ones you don't dare to say in fear

You are the words that you write
The movies you like to watch at night
And the restaurant you dine in at candlelight

You are the light before the sunrise, one of a
kind
Running to clear your mind
And the games that make you feel like a
mastermind

You are sweet and sour
Discussing politics for hours and hours
And the smell of my favorite flowers

You are perfect for me, and doubting it
Your messy room after trying to find an outfit
And watching TV shows while you eat

You are not liking to work in team
Holding me when all I want to do is scream

And a hot summer day with ice cream

You are a mystery worth discovering
Texting over calling
And deep conversations that should have been
my first warning

You are the pretty brown of your eyes I never
want to share
The curls in your hair
And the smile when I say something silly, the
one right there!

You are falling when you had too much to drink
Starting the morning with a cup of water before
you even blink
And your computer lock screen pink

You are everything no rhyme can describe
The match I never believed I would find
And the love of my life

9 789357 697101